Cranbury Public Library

23 North Main St., Cranbury, NJ 08512
(609) 655-0555   f: (609) 655-2858

www.CranburyPublicLibrary.org

D1373107

WHOSE BACK
IS THIS?

JOANNE RANDOLPH

PowerKiDS
press™
New York

Published in 2009 by The Rosen Publishing Group, Inc.
29 East 21st Street, New York, NY 10010

First Edition

Book Design: Julio Gil
Photo Researcher: Jessica Gerweck

Photo Credits: Cover, pp. 5, 7, 9, 11, 13, 15, 17, 19, 21, 23, 24 (top left, bottom left, bottom right) Shutterstock.com; p. 24 (top right) © www.istockphoto.com/Alexander Hafemann.

Library of Congress Cataloging-in-Publication Data

Randolph, Joanne.
  Whose back is this? / Joanne Randolph. — 1st ed.
     p. cm. — (Animal clues)
  Includes index.
  ISBN 978-1-4042-4454-2 (library binding)
  1. Body covering (Anatomy)—Juvenile literature. I. Title.
  QL941.R36 2009
  590—dc22

                                        2007047939

Manufactured in the United States of America

CONTENTS

What lives in the **desert** and has two **humps** on its back?

5

A camel lives in the desert and has two humps on its back.

Whose back is **bumpy** and orange and black?

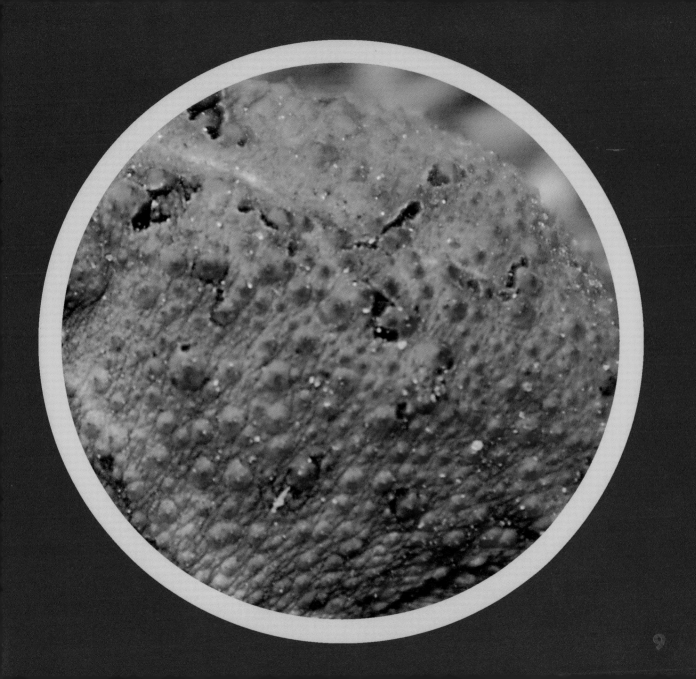

9

This toad's back is bumpy and orange and black.

11

Whose back has black and white **stripes**?

12

A zebra's back has black and white stripes.

Who has a shell with large bumps on its back?

This mountain tortoise has a shell with large bumps on its back.

What has a red back with
black spots all over it?

A ladybug has a red back with black spots all over it.

WORDS TO KNOW

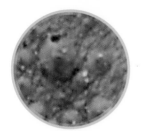

bumpy

desert

humps

stripes

INDEX

WEB SITES

Due to the changing nature of Internet links, PowerKids Press has developed an online list of Web sites related to the subject of this book. This site is updated regularly. Please use this link to access the list:
www.powerkidslinks.com/acl/back/